Love, Life, and Loss

A POETIC NARRATIVE

For my home

I LEFT WANDERING

Love, Life, and Loss

A POETIC NARRATIVE

CONTENTS

SHATTERED DREAMS

Heartbreak has spilled my ink,
My pen now writes of shattered dreams,
And each verse aches with a broken heart,
I fear to love again,
For it may silence my poetry forever.

A year has passed since they parted ways,
But her memory still echoes in his mind,
He longs to hold her once again,
But she's moved on and left him behind.

She's moved on, with someone new,
My heart aches with each beat,
As hers now beats to someone else's rhythm.
I can't escape the memories,
Of her lips on someone else's.
I thought I was her forever,
But forever was only temporary.

Here, take this ring back,
Our love has come to an end,"
He said with a broken heart.

"No, I can't take it back,
I want to keep it close,
As a reminder of what we had,
Of the love we shared and lost."

"Why keep a reminder of pain?"
He asked,

"Because you have a piece of my heart,
And I want to keep a piece of yours.

Every night she tells herself,
"I've moved on, he's in the past"
Yet every morning she wakes with a longing,
Hoping to see his name on her phone at last.

He broke down, pleading for one more chance
A familiar tune, I've heard it before
But this time, my resolve is strong
No more chances, to break my heart again.

The phone rang, my heart stopped
His voice on the other end
"I can't do this anymore"
The words ripped through my soul
A cry of pure agony tore from my throat
As my heart broke into smithereens
And the future I had planned
Crumbled before my eyes.

Don't worry, you'll find someone better,"
Words meant to soothe, but they cut deep,
I try to find solace in the reason for our end,
But my heart aches and my arms feel empty.

They asked me who my muse was,
I said "no one", but my heart ached,
For the one who inspired my art,
The one who left a permanent mark.

The spaces where you once were
Are now empty and cold,
I try to fill them with memories,
But they only make me feel old.

I try to forget you,
But your ghost haunts me still,
Leaving me with nothing,
But an empty space to fill.

Broken promises echo in my mind,
Reminding me of the love we left behind,
I thought our love was unbreakable,
But now it's just a memory, a fable.

I gave you my everything,
But you gave me nothing in return,
I thought forever was a promise,
But now it's just a lesson I've learned.

The last goodbye felt like a punch to the gut,
Leaving me gasping for air,
I never thought it would end like this,
But now all I have are tears.

I thought love was enough,
But it wasn't enough for you,
I'll keep the memories,
But my heart is broken in two.

I replay our memories,
Hoping to find a clue,
To understand why you left me,
And what I'm supposed to do.

But every replay just breaks me,
Leaving me with nothing but pain,
I thought our love was forever,
But now it's just a replay in my brain.

Only the right person's love to mend,
Piece by piece, I'll put myself together,
And find the strength to love again.

In her arms, he found a home,
A place where he felt complete,
But now that she's gone,
He's lost and incomplete.

With foolish pride, he said he'd find,
Someone better than her,
But as the rage and hurt subsided,
He saw the truth, a blur.

She was his everything,
His world and his light,
But in the heat of the moment,
He couldn't see what was right.

Now that she's gone,
He knows he made a mistake,
She was the only thing close to perfect,
And he'll never replace.

She said she couldn't live without him,
But she left him for another,
He asked her why she was leaving,
Her answer was like a dagger.

She said the other made her feel worthy,
And he could not compete,
His heart was broken and shattered,
On the shattered remains of their love, his heart
lie so incomplete.

He said they could no longer be together,
She warned him he'd regret it,
And now, her words echo in his mind,
A haunting reminder of what he'll never admit.

Years have flown by,
But her beauty remains unchanged,
His feelings for her still alive,
Though their love was estranged.

She appeared ethereal, like a goddess,
To the world, she may seem content,
But he alone could see the sorrow,
That lay beneath, hidden and bent.

His friend said she was happy now,
But he couldn't believe it was true,
"How do you know?" he asked,
"I've seen her pictures, she's smiling in them,"

"Don't be fooled by her art of deception,"
He replied, his voice laced with pain,
"She could always paint a beautiful smile,
But her heart still feels the same.

His words could have destroyed her,
But he kept them locked away,
The weight of what was left unspoken,
Was his heart's price to pay.

You said you'd stay with me forever,
Promises made to be broken,
But my heart is not a promise,
It's a love that should have been spoken.

I gave you my heart, my all,
But you left it incomplete,
My love for you unfulfilled,
My heart forever incomplete.

Memories of you haunt me,
Echoes of yesterday,
I thought love was forever,
But you proved me wrong in every way.

I paid the price for love,
With a broken heart in my hand,
But I wouldn't trade a single moment,
For the love that I had.

I gave you everything,
But it was all in vain,
You took my heart and left me,
Nothing but heartache and pain.

I thought love would heal,
But it left me in ruins,
My heart shattered and torn,
The aftermath of love's illusions.

I thought love was real,
But it was all an illusion,
You shattered my heart,
Leaving me with nothing but confusion.

I gave you my heart,
But you lost it along the way,
Now I'm left with nothing,
But memories of yesterday.

She betrayed the feelings she once held,
For someone new,
Leaving him heartbroken,
With nothing left but the blues.

I searched for solace in the Bible,
Memorizing its every word,
But its promises were empty,
Just another love that turned.

The feeling of déjà vu hit him,
Memories of her flooding back,
He longed to hold onto the moment,
But reality slapped him back.
He knew the end would be the same,
Leaving him with a feeling of chill.

Silent night, a weight of a thousand words,
My mind numb, my heart in aches,
I sipped the poison you gave me,
Not knowing it was a heartbreak.

I'll drown in sorrow and drink the poison,
My wounds may have healed, but scars remain,
I'm a fragile glass, shattered by love,
Held together by hands that shake with pain.
I fear if they let go, I'll fall apart,
Forever marked by a love that left its mark.

His nights were spent in a false paradise,
Images so vivid, he'd get lost in them,
If he could, he'd lose himself in sleep,
Forever escaping the heartache within.
But come morning, his dreams fade,
Reality comes crashing in,
He's stuck in a cycle of pain,
Forever searching for a way to begin.

She was a love forgotten,
A memory left behind,
Her memory a constant ache,
A pain etched deep in his mind.

I've felt too much,
Even when I tried to keep my heart closed,
Thought too much,
With a numb mind
I've given it my all, but it wasn't enough,
The world demands pain,
So I reach for the knife,
Wondering if my loss will be mourned,
As I try to escape the pain of love.

Heartbreak taught me to feel,
To know the depth of pain,
To understand the meaning of love,
And how it can leave a stain.
But through the tears, I've found hope,
And strength to carry on,
Heartbreak may have broken me,
But it won't keep me gone.

Heartbreak was my teacher,
It taught me to feel,
But grief is my companion,
As I learn to heal.
Memories linger on,
Like whispers in the night,
Guiding me towards,
The path to new light.
Though my heart is heavy,
And tears still flow,
I know with time,
Healing will come, and I'll grow.

GRIEF UNVEILED

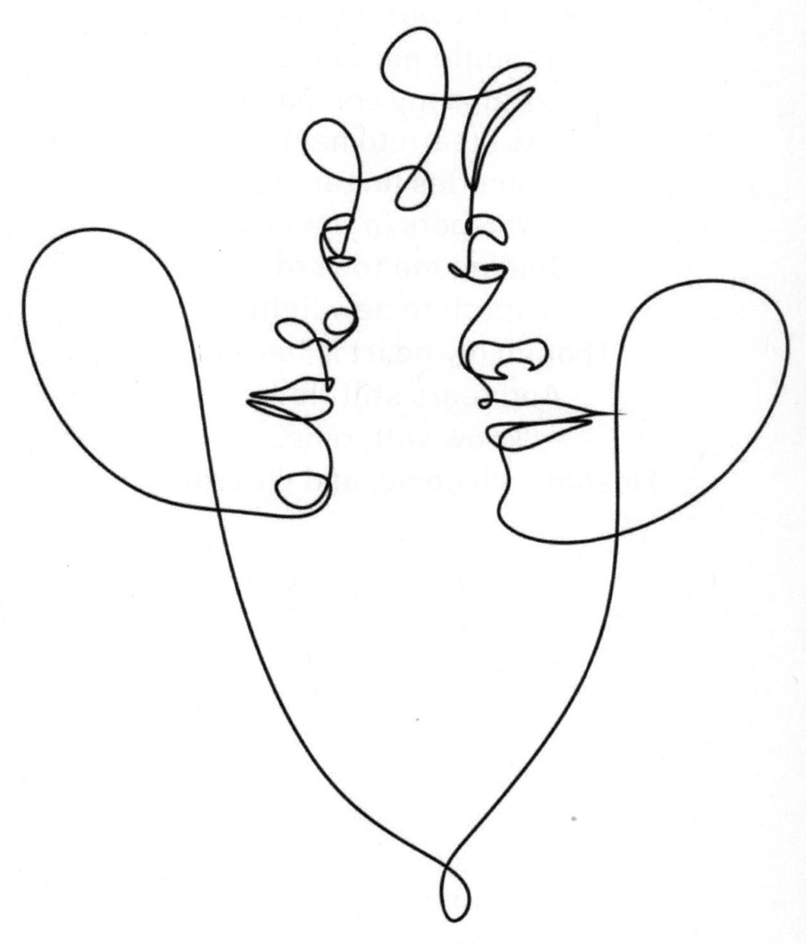

Grief has consumed me,
Everything seems dark,
My mind overwhelmed
by anger and depression,
My tongue tastes of ashes,
My body feels weak,
I search for a glimmer of light,
But all I can see is shadow.
Hope is my only anchor,
But will it guide me through this abyss?

I can't believe you're gone,
My mind still expects your return,
I keep holding on to memories,
Of a love that can't return.

I rage at the world,
For taking you away,
I curse the injustice,
Of a love that couldn't stay.

If only I had said this,
Or done that instead,
Maybe you'd still be here,
And I wouldn't be filled with dread.

I can feel the weight of your absence,
But I'll learn to carry it,
I'll accept that you're gone,
And honor our love with it.

I surrender to the grief
In the end, its all that's left
The love we shared is gone
But its memories will remain in our hearts
Forever.

They both hold the pen tightly
As they pour their grief onto the page
Her solace lies in the marks of charcoal
His, in the melody of words.

A year has passed since their bond broke
She no longer cares for his well-being
But all he longs for is just one touch
Of her breath against his cheek.

The sound of her laughter still echoes
in the halls of my mind
A haunting melody that
I cannot seem to shake
A constant reminder of what I have lost.

Grief is a fickle companion
One moment it's a whisper in my ear
The next, it's a scream that rips through me
Leaving me raw and exposed
But I hold on to it
For it is all that remains of her.

I thought my heart had turned to stone
But then love whispered my name
And I felt the cracks start to show
Hope seeped through like morning dew
A reminder that healing takes time
But love, like spring, will always find a way to bloom.

VULNERABLE LOVE

In the darkness, her love was a beacon
Guiding me through the night
Her messages, a sweet balm
Bringing joy and light to my life
And even the smallest moments of happiness
With her tasted like honey on my tongue.

Under the cloak of night,
We kept our vigil,
Two souls bound by love
Watching, waiting for the morning light
To chase away the darkness,
And bring us together again.

When her call went to voicemail,
She smiled, knowing that
Her love had finally won,
Giving him the peace to sleep,
And chasing away the insomnia
That had once plagued him.

I'll never fill the void left by him
Their love was etched in time,
I thought.
But she showed me a new path
One where I could take his place,
In her heart and her life.

"Why do you love me?" she whispered,
With doubts clouding her mind.
"Because your imperfections are what make you perfect to me,
Each scar and blemish a reminder of the strength you possess.
When I look at you, I see nothing but beauty and love radiating from within."
He replied, his words filled with conviction and adoration.

Her lips, adorned in red,
A canvas for his artist's touch,
A love story, written in every kiss
A masterpiece, forever etched in their hearts.

With every kiss, her lover breathed life into her
Transforming her mundane existence
Into a beautiful work of art
She radiated with the love he gave her.

He read her like an open book,
Bringing the words to life,
Completely immersing himself in her,
Forgetting about the world outside
Their love was a chapter so profound,
So breathtaking,
It was forever bookmarked in his heart.

Lonely for so long,
His lips yearned for a lover's touch,
But when she offered her own lips to him,
He hesitated no longer,
For he knew the sweetness he had been longing
for
Was finally within his reach.

He once detested the aroma of Mehendi
But when it wafted from her skin,
It became his most beloved scent
As it reminded him of the love and commitment
They shared, sealed with the traditional henna.

He was her safe haven,
A place where she could be herself
And he loved every inch of her,
Flaws and all.

She was his addiction,
A love he couldn't quit
The thought of her consumed him
And he was happy to be a slave to it.

His touch was electric,
Sending shivers down her spine
She couldn't get enough of him
And knew she never would.

Her laughter was music to his ears
And he couldn't help but smile
Whenever he heard it
Knowing that she was happy.

Their love was a work of art,
A masterpiece created by fate
And they knew it would last forever
For their love was truly great.

The solace he found in her embrace
Was a constant craving,
His nights incomplete without her touch
And his heart yearning for her love.

Distance tried to tear us apart,
Bit by bit, breaking our love.
But as my heart lay in pieces,
I knew I could not depart
For my love for her would forever be true,
No matter the space between us.
So I returned to her arms,
Where my heart truly belongs.

Her smile sets my heart aflame,
Her words, a symphony to my ears
In her eyes, I see my future-
A soul unspoiled by the cruelty of this world
Fated to be cherished by a faithful lover
A perfect match, written in the stars
Destined to find each other's hearts.

With a radiance that could light up the darkest
of skies,
She stood before him, a vision of beauty and
grace
Carrying within her the seed of their love,
A promise of new life and endless possibilities.
Her aura shone so brightly that all else around
her
Faded into insignificance, a goddess incarnate
Blessing him with her presence, her love, her all.

Tears streamed down her face,
As she pushed with all her might,
Her husband's hand tightly gripping hers,
Feeling the pain and fear alongside her.
But as their baby's cries filled the room,
Love and joy overwhelmed them,
Their hearts now forever intertwined,
By the little life they had brought into the world.

We share a silent understanding,
You and I.
I comprehend your silence,
For all that you want to say, my heart knows.
The way it's attuned to your fears,
That surface in the dead of night.
I wear my heart on my sleeve for you,
These unguarded walls have made me vulnerable,
But I find myself doing it without hesitation.
You took a piece of my soul when we were separated,
But I'll let you go, for your happiness is my priority.
For a lover's only wish is to see their beloved thrive.

A girl I met in my mind's eye,
Her beauty beyond compare,
I couldn't help but stare in awe.
With a smile that lit up the room,
She captured my heart without a care.
In her curves, I found my solace,
An ethereal creature, a goddess in my eyes.
But it was not just her looks that drew me in,
It was the way she moved, the way she inspired,
That made my heart race and my feet move,
In a love that was never forced,
But one that I fell into willingly and deeply.

A wanderer I am,
Roaming through my thoughts,
Searching for something true,
A love that cannot be bought.
Dreams and desires,
Guiding me on my quest,
But fear grips me tight,
Will I pass the test?
I run through the night,
Chasing after my heart's call,
Hoping to reach the end,
And find love standing tall.

He spoke of her beauty like Aphrodite,
Carved with such precision, a sight to see,
But she was hesitant to accept his words,
Doubting her own worth.
So, he told her that she no longer pleased him,
That her body was no longer a reflection of love.
But she took his words as a sign,
To leave and find herself,
Pursuing her dreams and finding self-love.
Though their love was lost,
He couldn't help but smile
Every time he saw her face on a magazine cover,
A wish fulfilled, an abandoned dream claimed.

He whispered her name,
As she lay beside him,
Her heart beating in synch with his
They were a symphony,
A perfect harmony,
Two souls intertwined,
Forever in love.

The way she tilted her head,
And her eyes lit up,
When he walked into the room,
Told him everything he needed to know
Without her ever having to say a word.

He traced the lines of her face,
Memorizing every curve,
Every freckle,
Every inch of her,
For he knew,
He would never get tired of looking at her.

She was the missing piece,
To his puzzle of life,
He never knew he needed,
But now that she was here,
He couldn't imagine living without her.

The pen in my hand,
A reflection of my heart
With every word I write
I pour out my love
For you, my dear
But insecurities creep in
Jealousy rears its ugly head
Longing for your touch
And moments we shared
But through it all
I am a poet
Forever in love with you.

POET'S MUSE

As one chapter closed
and another began,
His heart lay in ruins
But from the ashes,
a poet emerged.
Penning down their memories,
Transforming heartache into art.

Society's expectations weigh heavy,
A future as an engineer, my father's path.
But my heart beats to a different rhythm,
A poet's pen, my true passion.

The voice of doubt echoes in my mind,
"Your poetry is lacking, it's not worth a dime,"
But I won't let it discourage me,
For I know my words will one day set me free.

Some may question my intent,
Why I pour my heart onto these pages
For a love who cannot see the words
But it is through my writing
That I am able to show her
The depth of my adoration
And though I may not have a voice
My pen speaks volumes of my love.

The words once flowed freely,
From his pen to the page,
But now they are trapped,
In a prison of memories,
Of the love that once was,
And the love that now is.
He struggles to find the words,
To express emotions,
That overwhelms him,
But in her presence,
His words are silenced,
And all he can do is love.

"If I pen a novel, will you read it?"
He asked, filled with hope and longing
"Not now, finish your studies first"
She replied, crushing his dream for the moment.

With pen in hand, he scribbled away
Revising and rewriting until the words felt true,
His emotions poured onto the page,
As the ink in his pen ran dry
His love for her, immortalized in verse,
Recited at her funeral with a heart heavy,
A tear falling down his cheek,
A testament to the depth of his feelings.

He was asked about his heart's condition,
In response, he wrote her a poem,
Transcribing the broken pieces of his heart
Into ink on paper,
His words a reflection of the love and pain
That she had come to mean to him.

With each shattered love,
He poured his heart onto the page,
Transforming pain into verse,
Crafting a language all his own.
But it was with her,
The one who unlocked his heart,
That he truly became a poet.
She ignited a fire within him,
Fueling his passion and creativity,
And he knew that he would forever be
Bound to the words he wrote for her.

You are the inspiration behind my poetry
The source of my creative expression,
The one who ignites the fire in my soul
And brings my words to life.

My love for you is a fire
That burns bright and fierce,
But it also consumes me
With jealousy and fear.
I pen my thoughts on paper
Hoping to make sense of it all,
But my words cannot express
The depth of my love for you.

I write my love for you
In lines of poetry,
Each verse an ode to you
A reflection of my heart's melody.
But my words are not enough
To convey the depth of my feelings,
For my love for you is boundless
And my heart forever reeling.

The ink on my pages
Bleeds the story of our love,
The joy and the pain
The push and the shove.
I pour my heart out
In every verse and rhyme
Hoping that one day
You'll see the love in my lines.

I've been writing poetry
For as long as I can remember
But it was only when I met you
That my words became a treasure.
You inspire me to write
Of love, longing, and desire
And with every poem I pen
My love for you grows higher.

The words flow from my pen
Easily when I think of you
A love poem, a sonnet
A ballad, a haiku.
I try to capture
Every moment we share
But my words fall short
For my love for you is beyond compare.

I write of you in the dark
When all is quiet and still,
My pen dances across the page
As I pour my heart's fill.
I write of your smile
The way your laugh echoes true,
I write of the love I have for you
And all the things I wish to do.

I wrote my love for her in a poem,
But when I read it to her,
She said it was too simple,
It made me feel like a novice.

But I knew that my love for her
Could never be put into words,
So I put my pen down and took her in my arms
And whispered to her that my love was infinite.

He scribbled words on the pages
But they never seemed to convey
The depth of his love for her
So he turned to music and let the notes speak
For the words he couldn't say.

She was his shelter from the storm
The calm in the chaos of his mind
He wrote of her constantly
But even the most beautiful words
Couldn't do her justice.

I long to pen a book about you,
But my words seem insufficient
To capture the depth of my feelings.
I fear that in writing,
I'll lose you as my muse,
For the pages may reveal
How deeply your disregard cuts me.

"Why do you always write of heartache?"
They asked,
"Is it because you've known love's bitter taste?"
I simply smiled, for in my heart's dark space
Lies a love that time can never erase.

In the face of death, poetry took on a new light;
Each word, a testament to the beauty of life and love,
Crafted with care by a poet's steady hand,
A reflection of the soul, blessed by the heavens above.

The hues in my existence have faded,
Love's allure now gone.
Our shared moments now only a recollection
Of all that we were never meant to be.
My pen lies still, for my inspiration
has been lost
With a heavy heart, I must admit
Our love story has reached its final verse.

She walked into my life,
A ray of sunshine in a stormy sky,
She taught me to love again,
And with her, my poetry came alive.

We laughed and we loved,
Every moment felt like a fairytale,
But fate had other plans,
And she was taken from me.

The ink in my pen has dried,
My words are but echoes,
Of a love that once was,
A love that I can no longer feel.

The pages of my diary,
Are blank and bare,
For my heart is aching,
And my soul is in despair.
Without her, I am lost,
A poet without a muse,
Forever searching for the love,
That I once knew.

Empty pages stare back at me,
Mocking my attempts to write
Once filled with love and life,
Now nothing but a lonely blight.
My heart, once mended by her touch,
Now shattered, with nothing left to clutch.
The world around me fades to grey,
As I question my purpose each day.
With her gone, what is left to live for?
Only the emptiness of loss, and the pain that it bore.

ADRIFT IN EMPTINESS

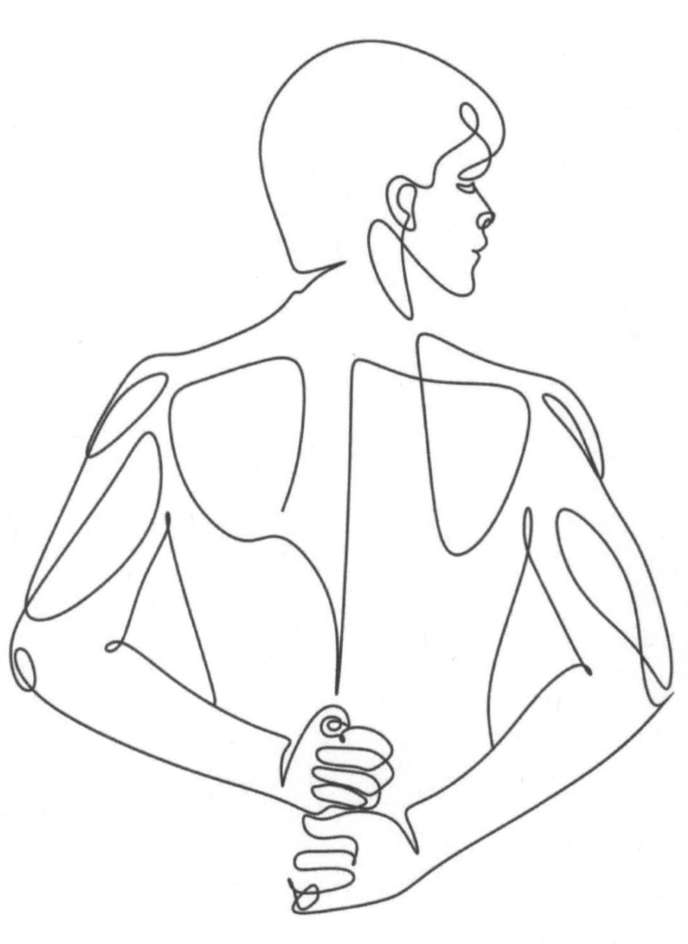

My heart is a graveyard,
Where love is buried deep,
And memories are the headstones
That mark where it sleeps.
My soul is a wasteland,
Where hope is long gone,
And the future is a mirage
That I can never hold on.
I am lost in the darkness,
With nothing to guide me,
And the weight of my sorrow
Is all that I can see.

Adrift in a sea of grief,
I wander aimlessly
My heart aching for a home
That I fear I've lost forever
Longing for a place of solace
But my memories have grown hazy
And my path is uncertain
With a heavy heart, I cry out
For guidance from a higher power.

I pray to you every day,
Kneeling before you in submission,
You are the first thought in my mind when starting anew,
But you never seem to help me,
I find myself lost and struggling,
My life spiraling into misery,
But I never lose faith in you,
Why don't you help me?
Why do you play with my life?
I cried out, questioning my deity,
But the answer came,
"I do not play with you, my child,
You are not a toy to be manipulated.
I am not controlling your strings,
But guiding your steps,
With a vision beyond your imagination,
Every step you take is already written in the book of fate."

She walked down the aisle,
Hand in hand with her soulmate,
But as she said her vows,
Her heart ached with grief.
For in her happiness,
She was leaving behind
The only home she'd ever known,
And the thought of it
Tore her apart.

Trapped in a loveless union,
Bound by societal expectations,
We lay in the same bed,
But our hearts are miles apart.
Fractured and broken,
We mask our pain with false smiles,
Conforming to the world's distorted view of love,
But deep down, our hearts ache for the ones we truly love.
Our arranged marriage has torn us away
from the embrace of true love.

They were once two halves of a whole,
But now they're just two pieces
Drifting further apart.
Each day feels like an eternity
As they struggle to find meaning
In a love that was once unbreakable.
Memories of their past linger
Haunting them with what could have been
As they come to terms with the fact
That their love story has come to an end.

As she watched him flirt with others,
Her heart filled with jealousy and rage,
She couldn't understand why he felt no jealousy,
When she was the one he claimed to love.
But he simply replied,
"I know that no matter what,
We are bound together by fate,
And our love will endure all that comes our way."
But her heart couldn't shake off the feeling,
That their love was being mocked by destiny.

Every step I take feels like a gamble,
With no guarantee of winning,
I'm lost in a maze of my own creation,
And I can't find my way out.

I've been searching for meaning,
But all I've found is emptiness,
I've been reaching for something,
But all I've grasped is air.

The weight of my sorrows is heavy,
And I'm struggling to bear it,
I've lost my way and I'm wandering,
With no hope of finding it again.

She played the game of life with skill and grace,
Strategizing every move with care,
But in the end, it was Death who claimed the prize,
Stealing her king and leaving her in despair.
Though she fought with all her might,
The game was lost before it even began,
Leaving her feeling empty and alone,
As she mourned the loss of her one true love.

In the end, it didn't matter
How much love I gave or received
How many battles I won or lost
All that was left was the void
The emptiness that consumed me
As I lay dying, I realized
That in the grand scheme of things
I was just a fleeting moment
A mere blip on the radar of existence
And with my last breath, I let go
Embracing the darkness that called to me
For in death, I finally found my END.

FINAL FAREWELL

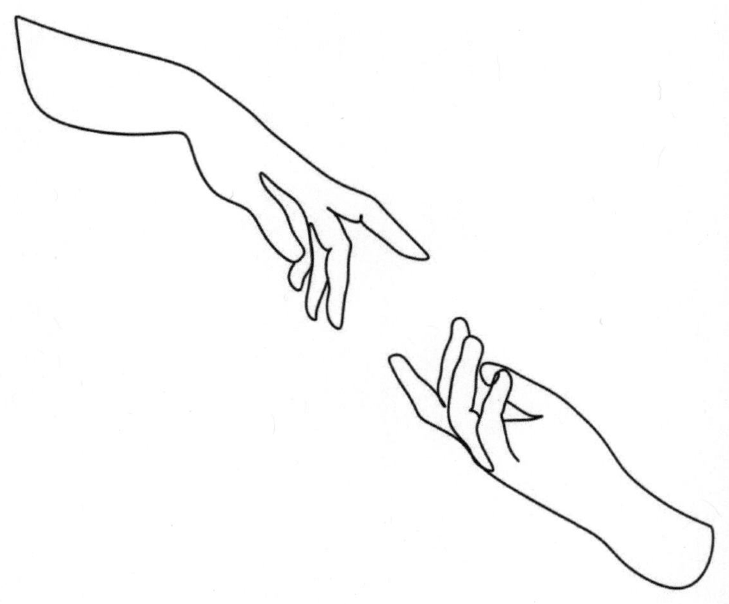

As he lay dying, his pen in hand,
With his final breath, he wrote his last command.
A masterpiece, his life's labor,
A legacy to leave, a final favor.

Through love and loss, he'd found his voice,
And in ink, he'd made his final choice.
To leave behind a work of art,
That would speak of his life, his heart.

With her words, "Magnum Opus," ringing in his ears,
He closed his eyes, and let out a final tear.
For though his life was over, his story lived on,
In the pages of his book, forever strong.

He'd found his purpose, his one true goal,
To create, to love, to touch the soul.
And as his life came to an end,
He found peace in the knowledge that his work would transcend.

Printed by Libri Plureos GmbH in Hamburg,
Germany